PET BIRDS

Questions and Answers

by Christina Mia Gardeski

CAPSTONE PRESS
a capstone imprint

Pebble Plus is published by Capstone Press,
1710 Roe Crest Drive, North Mankato, Minnesota 56003
www.mycapstone.com

Library of Congress Cataloging-in-Publication Data
Cataloging-in-Publication data is on file with the Library of Congress.
ISBN 978-1-5157-0354-9 (library binding)
ISBN 978-1-5157-0361-7 (paperback)
ISBN 978-1-5157-0367-9 (eBook PDF)

Editorial Credits
Carrie Braulick Sheely and Alesha Halvorson, editors; Kayla Rossow, designer;
Pam Mitsakos, media researcher; Gene Bentdahl, production specialist

Photo Credits
Alamy: Ashley Cooper, 4-5, Elena Abduramanova, 15, Eudyptula, 13, kungverylucky, 7,
Tracy Starr, 11, Ulyana Vyugina, 19, VladisChern, 1, 22, Yuangeng Zhang, cover, zhuda, 21,
Zurijeta, 17; Thinkstock: einegraphic, 9, moodboard, 10

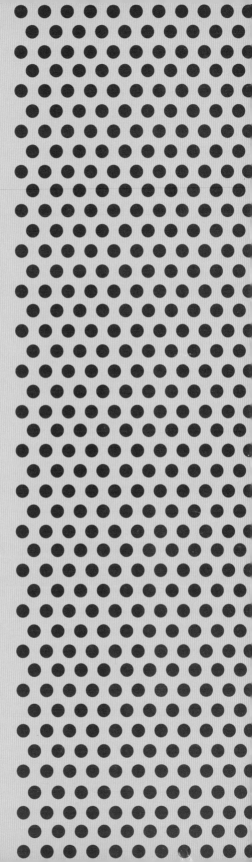

Note to Parents and Teachers

The Pet Questions and Answers set supports national curriculum standards for science related
to life science. This book describes and illustrates pet birds. The images support early readers
in understanding the text. The repetition of words and phrases helps early readers learn new
words. This book also introduces early readers to subject-specific vocabulary words, which are
defined in the Glossary section. Early readers may need assistance to read some words and
to use the Table of Contents, Glossary, Read More, Internet Sites, Critical Thinking Using the
Common Core, and Index sections of the book.

Printed in China.
022016   007713

Table of Contents

Who Wants a Bath?

My bird!

Birds love to stay clean.

They splash in bird baths.

Birds preen their feathers

with their beaks.

Do Birds Have Ears?

Birds' ears are hard to see.

They are hidden by feathers.

Birds have one big ear hole

behind each eye. Most birds

can hear very well.

Why Do Birds Sing?

Birds sing to talk to other birds.

They sing to tell where they live

and to show off. Many birds

sing early in the morning.

Can My Bird Make Me Sneeze?

Birds shed their feathers and grow
new ones. This is called molting.
Tiny feather bits called dander
can make you sneeze.

What Do Birds Eat?

Birds eat food called pellets.

They like fresh fruits and vegetables.

Keep their bowls away from

droppings. Give them

clean water every day.

Where Can I Keep My Bird?

Pet birds can live indoors in a
big cage. Line it with clean paper.
Set perches high and low.
Add swings, ladders, and bells
for play.

Can I Train My Bird?

Birds are smart. Some can be
trained to rest on your finger
and do simple tricks.
Others can learn to talk.

Can I Let My Bird Out of Its Cage?

It is healthy for a bird to be outside its cage. But birds can get hurt flying indoors. Make a safe bird playroom. Hide cords. Turn off fans. Close all windows and doors.

Does My Bird Need a Buddy?

Birds need friends just like you do!

Talk and play with your bird every day.

Let it hop on your hand. Bring another

bird home if you can.

Glossary

dander—tiny bits of feathers or skin

dropping—bird waste

molt—to lose feathers regularly

pellet—a small, dry, rounded piece of bird food

perch—a rod on which a bird rests

preen—to make the feathers neat and clean with the beak

shed—to let something fall or drop off

Read More

Graubart, Norman D. *My Bird.* Pets Are Awesome!
New York: PowerKids Press, 2014.

Dubke, Karon. *Pet Parrots Up Close.* Pets Up Close.
North Mankato, Minn.: Capstone Press, 2015.

West, David. *Pets in the Home.* Nora the Naturalist's Animals.
Mankato, Minn.: Smart Apple Media, 2014.

Internet Sites

FactHound offers a safe, fun way to find Internet sites related to this book. All of the sites on FactHound have been researched by our staff.

Here's all you do:

Visit *www.facthound.com*

Type in this code: 9781515703549

Super-cool stuff! Check out projects, games and lots more at
www.capstonekids.com

Critical Thinking
Using the Common Core

1. What are things you can do to make it safe for your pet bird to fly indoors? (Key Ideas and Details)

2. Why do you think birds are good family pets? (Integration of Knowledge and Ideas)

Index